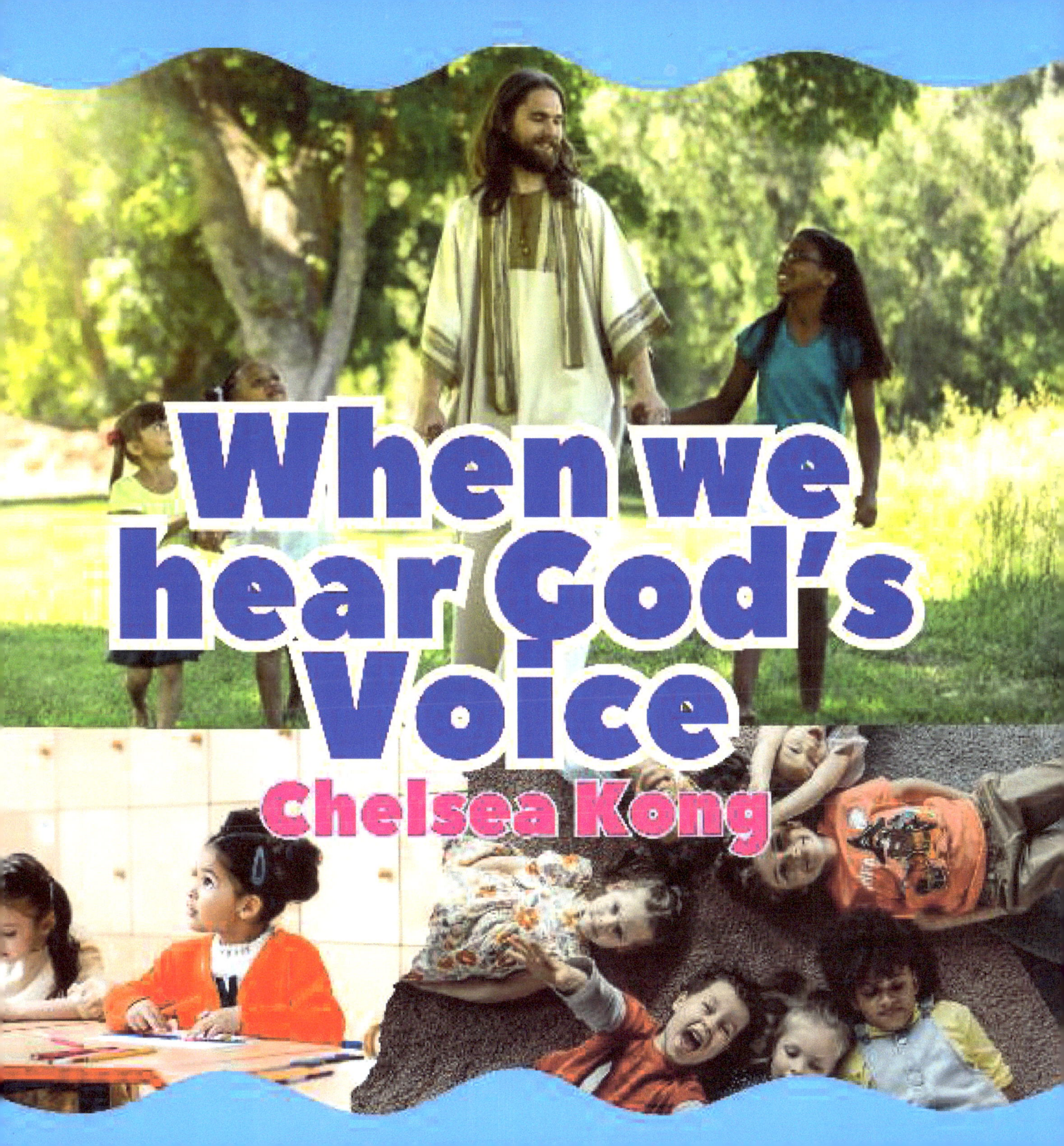

© 2024-2025 Chelsea Kong

All rights reserved. All images used in this book are licensed copies from their respectful owners including Canva, Unsplash, AI Image Gen, others. This book or any portion thereof may not be reproduced or used in any manner whatsoever without the express written permission of the publisher except for the use of brief quotations in a book review.

Printed in 2024-2026, Made in Toronto, Canada
ISBN: 978-1-998335-69-5
E=Book ISBN: 978-1-998335-70-1
Library and Archives Canada

I pray that this book will be a blessing to you.

Know what the Bible says.
It is God's Word.

Go to church and watch teachings about the Bible.

Look for a place.
Make to be alone with Him.

**Talk to Holy Spirit every day.
Listen and obey Him.
He will teach you about Jesus.**

Let Jesus talk to you. He will teach you.

Jesus and Holy Spirit will tell you things.
He shares through people too.

A new song, dance, art, game, drama, movie, book, and more.

God, Jesus, and Holy Spirit share about the future.

He tells us through places, things, and unseen things.

**Keep what He says and do it.
Write, draw, and record.**

Remember and practice the new things He gives you.

You will need to use what He gives you to do His work.

Share what the Lord and the Holy Spirit tell you to share.

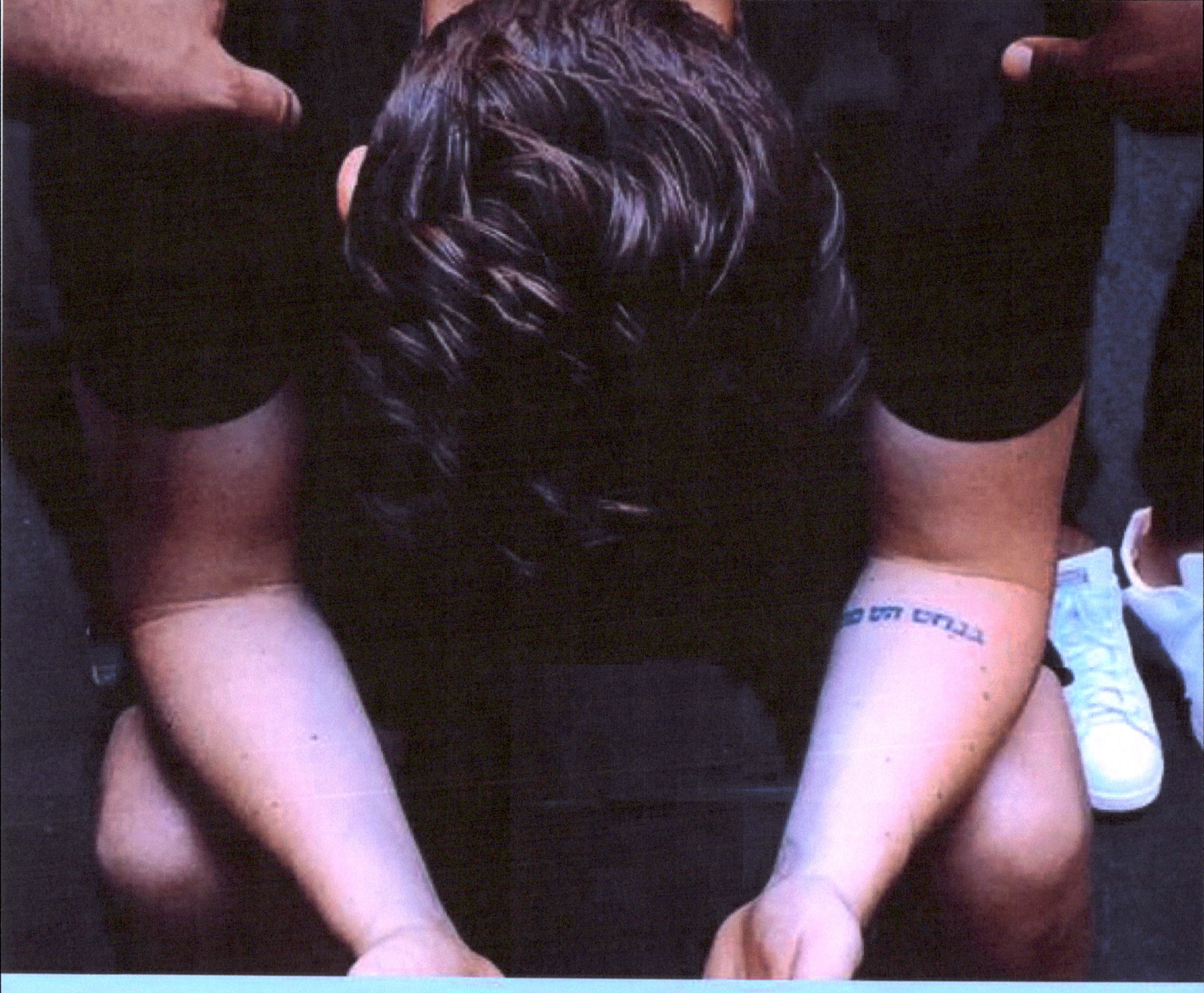

Your spirit becomes thankful and your faith strong.

SALVATION PRAYER

God, I know I sinned against you. Forgive me for the wrong that I have done. I believe that Jesus Christ died on the cross for me. That He rose from the grave so that after three days. I can have His long-lasting life. Come into my heart to be my Lord and Savior. I choose to turn away from my sins and I choose to follow you. Lead me to walk with you. Keep me safe and teach me your ways. Stop every bad thing in my life that has an open door to hurt me. Close those doors. Holy Spirit, fill me now in Jesus' name. Amen.

BAPTISM IN THE HOLY SPIRIT

Jesus, you are the one that fills me with Your Spirit. Come Holy Spirit and come into my life and fill me to overflow with Your presence. Come with your fire too. Thank you for the gift of tongues in Jesus' name. Amen.

Open your mouth and let the words come out that God gives you. It will be words that you don't know what they mean. You can ask God what it means. You need to let Him talk through you every day to grow this gift.

He will bring you closer to God and you will know Jesus more. You will have power from God to do great things and know things.

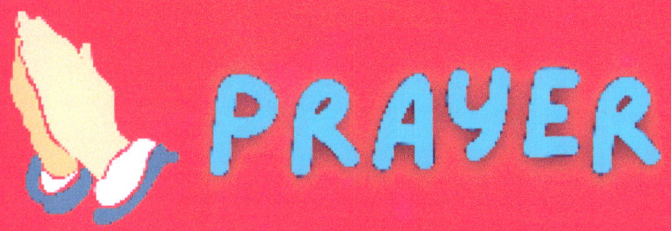

PRAYER

Thank you, Father, for teaching me how to hear your voice. Thank you, Jesus and the Holy Spirit, for sharing with me. Thank you, that you are my friend too. Open my ears to hear you more and more and to follow you. Let me see visions and dreams. Teach me what they mean. I want to see and know you more in Jesus' name. Amen.

Message from the Author

Thank you for reading this book. I hope you can leave a nice review to encourage me to write more books. God made us to live in His presence. That means to be with Him every day and all the time. He is with us in everything that we do. Jesus and the Holy Spirit want us to speak to them, too. When we are close to them, our life will become blessed. We will become like Jesus. The devil will fight, but he won't win. He will keep trying, but we need to keep stopping his attacks. God's Word is our sword and shield to keep us safe from harm. It opens the way for us to get out of danger. It teaches us how to command the angels to work for us to do God's plan.

OTHER PRODUCTS

- Knowing God
- How to Hear God's Voice
- New Life in Jesus
- Loving Israel
- God's Gifts/Spiritual Talents
- Meeting God
- Word Power
- Fruit of the Spirit
- The Tabernacle
- Bride for Jesus
- A Life of Prayer
- Live Free
- Who am I in Jesus
- Walk in Love
- God's Favor
- Man of God
- Woman of God
- How to Use Money
- God's Wisdom
- Fasting
- See Jerusalem and Bethany
- First Fruit Offering
- Feast of Trumpets
- Day of Atonement
- Feast of Tabernacles
- Counting the Omer
- Festival of Lights
- Glory, Presence, and Holy Spirit
- Live in God's Presence
- Pentecost
- See Galilee, Nazareth, and Tiberias
- Hear God Speak
- Knowing Jesus
- Knowing Holy Spirit
- A Healthy Life and Healthy Life Work Book
- Smokey the Cat
- Passover Unleavened Bread
- Resurrection Life
- The Blessing
- Revival
- Chelsea Learns Hebrew
- Thanksgiving

OTHER PRODUCTS

Give Thanks
Jesus Birth
Loving Jesus: Bride and Groom
Proverbs 31 Woman
ABC of People in the Bible
Colours in the Bible
Breakthroughs
Open Doors
The Seven Spirits of God
Numbers in the Bible
Aglee the Eagle
An Eagle's Life
Chelsea Learns Numbers in Hebrew
ABC's of Faith
Feast of Purim
A Royal Life
Family Day
Family Blessings
Chinese New Year
Loving Jesus for Children
Worship

Pandas
Canada
Celia's Birthday
Animal Stories
Eagles
Fun in West Caribbean
Courtroom of of God
Fun in Yellowknife
Windsor
Tecumseh
Fragrances in the Bible
Fun in Alberta
Fun in Labrador
Fun Facts about Japan
Canada's Government

Coming Soon
A Payroll Career
Sports I love

OTHER PRODUCTS

Devotionals
31 Day Devotional

Inspirational/Other
Chelsea's Psalms and Poems
Your Daily Meal: Chelsea's Photo Album
Chelsea's Psalms and Poems 2
Travel West Caribbean
Chelsea's Recipes
Chelsea's Psalms and Poems 3
Travel to Yellowknife
Travel to Alberta
Travel to Labrador
Travel to Petra

Puzzle Books
Biblical Puzzle Book Vol 1-5
Bible Puzzles for Young Children Book 1-3
Biblical Puzzle for Children Books 1 5
Chelsea's Bible Puzzles

OTHER PRODUCTS

Teaching Series

How to Hear God's Voice Teaching Guide & Audio Book
Relationship with God, Jesus, Holy Spirit Guide
Knowing God, Jesus, Holy Spirit Guide & Audio Book
Flowing in the Prophetic

Teaching (Non Sale on my website)
Purim
Passover
Resurrection

Coming soon

Travel Petra
Chelsea's Psalms and Poems4

BOOK REVIEWS

More books on Amazon, Kobo, and Barnes and Noble, Smashwords, and IngramSpark.
https://chelseak532002550.wordpress.com/

More books on Amazon, Kobo, and Barnes and Noble, Smashwords, and IngramSpark.
https://www.amazon.com/author/chelseakong

Please leave a review and share with friends to help the author continue to write more books to reach more readers. Thank you so much for your support.

Review!

About
CHELSEA KONG

She is a writer, creative arts and digital media artist, skilled administration and certified PCP (Payroll Compliance Professional), and podcaster. Chelsea also served in a variety of roles, from audiovisual, photography, to assisting on the worship team, and ministry team. She also has a passion for families being united.

Chelsea has been a guest on Unity Live Radio, The Lady Tracey Show, and How to Live for Christ and is highly recommended by a Proud Christian blog. She is also a guest blogger. A few of her books have been featured in YourAuthorHub, etc. She graduated from Hotel and Restaurant Management, Digital Media Arts, Office Administration, Payroll Compliance Professional, and experience working with children. Chelsea lives in Toronto, Canada. She mainly writes children's books, stories, bridal writing, poems, lyrics for songs, words of encouragement, blessings, prayers, and jokes. The author of How to Hear the Voice of God, the Bridal Collection, Knowing God, etc. She also has her own Bible Puzzle books and other inspired products. Her podcast channel is called Chelsea K on Anchor, Spotify, and iTunes.

Please check my website to find out more:
https://chelseak532002550.wordpress.com/

www.ingramcontent.com/pod-product-compliance
Lightning Source LLC
Chambersburg PA
CBHW041413010526

44107CB00016B/1151